WORDS BY
HANNAH
ANDERSON

THE
WORLD
GOD MADE

PICTURES BY
NATHAN ANDERSON

B&H
kids
Brentwood TN

In the world God made . . .

THE SKY is like a great big tent
so bright and blue and radiant!
It's stretched above the mountains high
and filled with birds and things that fly.

Sometimes the clouds hang dark and low
then noisy winds begin to blow.
But do not worry. Do not fear—
the One who made them will come near.

And in a moment, quick and strong,
he'll send the sun to come along.

His light will chase the dark away
and shine throughout the world God made.

THE EARTH is rugged, rich, and firm.
It's full of rocks and dirt and worms.
So even things that stomp around
can never move or shake the ground.

The mountains grow
up large and steep
while valleys drop
down wide and deep.
But next to things
so big and tall,
we often feel
a little small.

Still, even if the earth might quake,
the God who made it will not break.

Go hike and climb and jump all day
as you explore the world God made.

THE RIVERS rush and swirl around
while springs erupt from underground.
And from the hills, sweet waters flow
to all those thirsty down below.

This water is
for all the world,
for plants and people,
beast and bird.
But if we drink
and drink so much,
how can there be
enough for us?

Our God has so much more in store
with mercies rich forevermore.

He pours his blessings out like rain
to shower all the world God made.

Now, PLANTS are miracles from dirt:
just put a seed into the earth,
and when the sun and rain combine,
your seed will sprout into a vine.

This vine will grow a vegetable
or fruit so very plentiful.
But what about a food that's new—
that smells a little strange to you?

Just taste and see that God is good—
he fills the hungry with rich food.

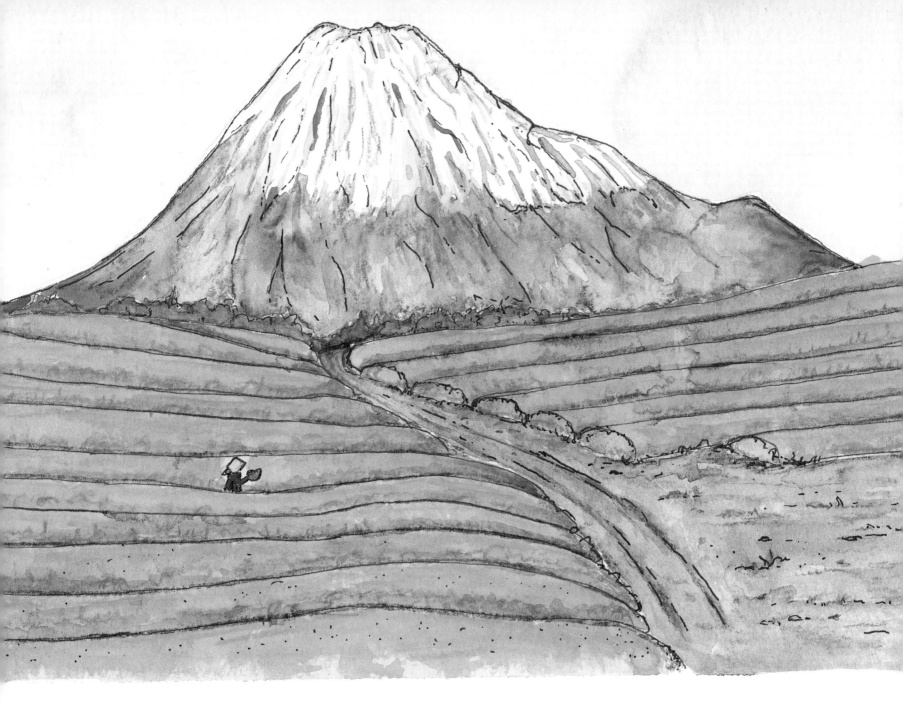

Then bow your head and learn to pray.
Give thanks for all the world God made.

THE STORKS have trees, the goats have hills,
and zebras graze among the fields.
And even if they hunt or stray,
the lions have a place to stay.

But still, the birds will leave their nest,
fly south and north and east and west.
They'll go to places far from home;
they might get scared all on their own.

But Someone's watching over them;
our God will bring them back again.

And he will lead you on your way
to guide you through the world God made.

THE SEA is full of things that swim,
that move about with scales and fins.
From shark and ray to octopus
and turtles from Galapagos.

But oceans can feel very deep
when filled with things that float and creep.
The sea holds secrets down below
and many things we do not know.

But questions are completely free—
God loves your curiosity!

So take your boat across the waves
to learn about the world God made.

THE SUN shines brightly through the day,
and by its light, we'll work and play.
But when it's time for bed and rest,
the sun dips quickly in the west.

Then all the stars from outer space
line up around the moon in place.
But nighttime can feel awfully long
with hours and hours before the dawn.

So listen closely. Try to learn:
the One who makes the heavens turn

is with you until darkness fades,
protecting all the world God made.

THIS WORLD has wonders large and small;
our God's the one who made them all.
And everywhere you look around,
both good and glory can be found.

A million strange and splendid things
to make you laugh, to make you sing.
So celebrate and praise his name
for all that's in the world God made.

AUTHOR'S NOTE:

The World God Made is a retelling of Psalm 104 that invites children and the adults in their lives to explore the natural world around them. Paralleling the order and structure of the original psalm, each stanza focuses on a specific feature of the natural world, as well as introducing a question or challenge that might originate from a child's experience of it. Perhaps it's traveling to a new place or trying a new food; maybe it's lying awake in the dark or wondering about all that we don't know. Each conflict embodies the fears and worries common to life on this earth. The stanzas resolve with a truth about God's character to comfort the child and give them the confidence they need to venture out. I trust these truths will comfort you as well.

ARTIST'S NOTE:

Psalm 104 tells of the breadth of God's creation. I wanted to honor that largesse in my art by celebrating the diversity and variety of life on all seven continents. Each of the seven stanzas tells the story of life in a different part of the world God made. I chose watercolor because of the soft and pleasing nature of the colors. (And I was literally painting with water.) Then I went back in and added details and highlights with watercolor pencils and ink. As you read, encourage your child to observe each picture closely. You'll find smaller stories and details to enhance your enjoyment of both the poetry and illustrations. Look for repeated patterns, animals that show up in multiple ecosystems, and repeating motifs. Further information about the locations, wildlife, and flora is available free online at sometimesalight.com/shop.

Text copyright © 2023 by Hannah Anderson. Art copyright © 2023 by Nathan Anderson. Published by B&H Publishing Group, Brentwood, Tennessee.
978-1-0877-6980-6 Dewey Decimal Classification: C550. Subject Heading: BIBLE. O.T. PSALMS 104 \ NATURE \ EARTH
Printed in Dongguan, Guangdong, China, November 2022   1 2 3 4 5 6 • 26 25 24 23 22